Garfield [illegible] Himself

by

JIM DAVIS

Ballantine Books · New York

A Ballantine Book
Published by The Random House Publishing Group

Published in the United States by Ballantine Books, an imprint of The Random House Publishing Group, a division of Random House, Inc., New York, and simultaneously in Canada by Random House of Canada Limited, Toronto.

This work was originally published in three separate titles: as *Here Comes Garfield, Garfield on the Town,* and *Garfield Gets a Life.*
HERE COMES GARFIELD is based on the television special produced by United Media Productions. Jay Poynor, Executive Producer, in association with Lee Mendelson-Bill Melendez Productions, written by Jim Davis. (© 1982 Paws, Inc.)
GARFIELD ON THE TOWN is based on the television special produced by United Media Productions. Jay Poynor, Executive Producer, in association with Lee Mendelson-Bill Melendez Productions, written by Jim Davis and Lorenzo Music. (© 1983 Paws, Inc.)
Designed and created by Jim Davis
Illustrated by Mike Fentz and Kevin Campbell
GARFIELD GETS A LIFE is based on the television special written by Jim Davis, directed by Phil Roman, in association with United Media-Mendelson Productions. (© 1991 Paws, Inc.)
Created by Jim Davis
Story by Jim Davis
Adapted by Kim Campbell and Gary Barker
Illustrations by Paws, Inc.

www.ballantinebooks.com

Library of Congress Catalog Card Number: 2004092855

ISBN-10: 0-345-47805-3
ISBN-13: 978-0-345-47805-4
Manufactured in China

First Edition: July 2004

9 8 7 6 5 4

HERE COMES GARFIELD

BY: JIM DAVIS

TWEET

TWEET
TWEET

TWEET!

CRASH!!!
SQUAWK!

BARK!

THUMP!

GOOD MORNING, ODIE

YOU'RE NOT GOING TO LIVE TO SEE YOUR NEXT BIRTHDAY

I HATE DOGS

GARFIELD

GARFIELD

GARFIELD

ARFIELD

RATS... MY OWNER MUST STILL BE LOLLING AROUND IN BED
GARFIELD

IT'S HARD TO FIND GOOD HELP THESE DAYS
GARFIELD

DO DEE DO
DEE DO

HELLO, ANYBODY THERE?

PLIP!

TAPPITY! TAPPITY!

RATTLE
RATTLE
RATTLE

MMMPH

ARRRRGH!

GOOD MORNING,
SUNSHINE

WELCOME TO ANOTHER
FUN-FILLED DAY WITH,
YOUR FAVORITE PET

I SUPPOSE
YOU WANT
BREAKFAST
THAT WOULD
BE GREAT

I'M SO HAPPY
TO OWN A CAT

I COULD
THROW UP

WHAT WOULD YOU LIKE FOR BREAKFAST, GARFIELD?

I'LL HAVE A CUP OF COFFEE, A DANISH AND THE MORNING PAPER

OKAY, ONE BOWL OF CAT FOOD COMING RIGHT UP!

NOBODY LISTENS ANYMORE

YOU KNOW, GARFIELD. I WOULDN'T HAVE TO FEED YOU SO MUCH IF YOU WOULD PROVIDE FOR YOURSELF
GARFIELD

WHY DON'T YOU CHASE MICE LIKE OTHER CATS?
GARFIELD

SHOW ME A GOOD MOUSER AND I'LL SHOW YOU A CAT WITH BAD BREATH
GARFIELD

EXCUSE ME

I'M NOT KNOWN FOR MY COMPASSION

SNIFF
GARFIELD

THE BOUQUET LEAVES SOMETHING TO BE DESIRED
GARFIELD

GARFIELD

BARK!

WHY DON'T YOU BOYS GO OUTSIDE TO FIGHT

YEOW!!

WHY YOU LITTLE...!

HEY, ODIE, WANT TO HAVE SOME FUN?

LET'S CATCH THE DOG NEXT DOOR AND WRING HIS TINY NECK

COME HERE, HONEY BUN, COME TO DADDY

WHAT'S THE MATTER, HONEY BUN? DID THAT MEAN OLD CAT AND DOG NEXT DOOR TRY TO HURT YOU AGAIN?

I THOUGHT SO

THERE ARE THOSE PESKY VARMINTS!

GET OFF MY PROPERTY, DANG YA!

DON'T COME ANOTHER STEP CLOSER!

THAT DOES IT!

REBA, REBA! THAT CAT AND DOG ARE IN MY YARD AGAIN. WHERE'S MY STICK?

IT'S RIGHT BESIDE YOU WHERE YOU ALWAYS KEEP IT, DEAR

I KNOW THAT

HERE KITTY, COME HERE DOGGY

I WANT TO PET YOU...

...WITH MY STICK!

CRASH

WELL, JUST LOOK AT YOU, HUBERT... POTTED AGAIN! HEH, HEH, HEH, HEH

DAGNABBIT, REBA, CAN'T YOU SEE I'VE BEEN ASSAULTED BY THOSE PESKY VARMINTS. BRING ME THE PHONE!

YOU'VE DONE IT THIS TIME! I'M GOING TO FIX YOUR WAGONS ONCE AND FOR ALL!!

HELLO, CITY POUND? THIS IS HUBERT ON MAIN STREET. I'VE GOT A COUPLE OF CUSTOMERS FOR YOU

SEND A TRUCK RIGHT OVER

CITY POUND

WHAT TOOK YOU SO LONG?

GET THAT CAT AND THAT DOG! TAKE 'EM AWAY!

UH, OH, IT'S THE CITY POUND!

COME ON, LET'S GET OUT OF HERE!

ODIE! MAKE A BREAK FOR IT!

BHD-2U2

ODIE, YOU'RE SO STUPID YOU DON'T EVEN KNOW YOU'RE IN BIG TROUBLE!

I MAY NEVER SEE YOU AGAIN

HD-2U2

OH, WELL, GOOD RIDDANCE, ODIE. I NEVER LIKED YOU MUCH ANYWAY!
POUND

TEN THOUSAND DOGS IN THIS CITY AND I HAVE TO LIVE WITH TWEEDLE DEE THE WONDER DUMMY

UH OH! GARFIELD WANTS IN!
KNOCK-
KNOCK-
NEWS

BAM!-
BAM!

BAM!
BAM!

WHEN I WANT IN, I WANT IN **NOW**!

OBOY, AM I BORED

I GUESS I MISS ODIE. IT'S HARD TO BELIEVE I COULD MISS SOMEONE WHO STARES AND SLOBBERS ALL AT THE SAME TIME...

... SOMEONE WHO HAS TO TURN AROUND THREE TIMES BEFORE LYING DOWN...

... SOMEONE WHO DRINKS OUT OF THE TOILET

I REMEMBER WHEN ODIE AND I WERE JUST PUPPY AND KITTEN

Z

BARK!

SNIFF, SNIFF

WHAT'S THAT? C-COULD IT BE?

NAW, IT COULDN'T...

YES, IT COULD...

NO, IT ISN'T...

YES, IT'S...

FOOD!

THAT HURTS!

NO SWEAT, SARGE. I'LL TAKE THAT MACHINE GUN NEST OUT WITH MY TRUSTY BAZOOKA HERE

SO THIS IS WHAT IT FEELS LIKE TO BE POTATO SALAD

RHETT, RHETT. WHATEVER SHALL I DO? WHEREVER SHALL I GO?

TAKE ME TO YOUR LEADER, EARTHLING, OR I'LL ATOMIZE YOUR FACE

PTUI

WELL, IF IT ISN'T NATURE'S MOST PERFECT FOOD...

LASAGNA!

WHERE HAVE YOU BEEN ALL MY LIFE, MON CHERIE?

YOU KNOW I CAN'T RESIST YOU WHEN YOU WEAR GARLIC IN YOUR MEAT SAUCE

WOULD YOU LIKE TO COME TO MY PLACE FOR DINNER?

OH, VERY WELL, I'LL JUST...

HAVE DINNER RIGHT HERE

I'M BORED, BORED-BORED-BORED-BORED-BORED-BORED-BORED-BORED. I AM BORED

THAT'S IT! I'M GOING DOWN TO THE CITY POUND AND I'M GOING TO BREAK ODIE OUT OF THERE!

LOOK OUT, POUND! HERE COMES GARFIELD!

CITY POUND

PSST, HEY BUDDY, YOU GOT ANY CIGARETTES ON YOU?

WHAT KIND OF A QUESTION IS THAT?

I DON'T KNOW. IT'S JUST SOMETHING YOU'RE SUPPOSED TO ASK

BACK OFF, ODIE. YOU'RE THE REASON I'M IN THIS FIX

HEY, HEY, FELLA, TAKE IT EASY ON THE MUTT

WHO ARE YOU, AND WHAT BUSINESS IS IT OF YOURS, ANYWAY?

I'M FAST EDDIE AND THIS IS MY ASSOCIATE, FLUFFY

AND IF YOU MUST KNOW, YOU SHOULD BE NICE TO THE MUTT THERE BECAUSE HE'S THE NEXT TO GO

GO WHERE?

HEH, HEH, HEH! LOOK PAL, THIS AIN'T THE GOOD SHIP LOLLIPOP, HERE

THIS IS THE CITY POUND. IF NO ONE COMES TO CLAIM US IT'S ...

...YOU KNOW WHAT I MEAN?

HOW LONG DOES ODIE HAVE?

'TILL DAWN

LET'S CHANGE THE SUBJECT

SURE, YOU WANT TO TALK ABOUT NEEDLEPOINT?

THAT WOULD BE NICE

AH, SHUT UP!

YOU'LL HAVE TO EXCUSE MY ASSOCIATE. IT WAS HIS LACK OF SMARTS THAT GOT HIM HERE TO BEGIN WITH...

...COULDN'T BE HOUSEBROKEN

AND YOU?
I WAS, YOU MIGHT SAY, BETWEEN OWNERS WHEN THEY CAUGHT ME ROAMING THE STREETS

THERE ARE MANY INTERESTING STORIES BEHIND WHY THESE PETS ARE HERE

FIDO THERE WAS NOT ON A LEASH, ROCKY BEAT UP A NEIGHBORHOOD DOG

CHARLOTTE SHARPENED HER CLAWS...ON A KING EDWARD V DIVAN

AND WEIRD LONNIE IS IN HERE FOR IMPERSONATING A MOOSE

WELL, IT'S TIME TO HIT THE SACK

SACK? WHAT SACK?

THAT SACK!

COME ON, ODIE, LET'S GET SOME SLEEP

DON'T WORRY, OLD BUDDY, YOU'LL BE OKAY

I NEVER KNEW I'D HAVE TO SAY, SO LONG

CLANK!

NO! YOU CAN'T TAKE ODIE AWAY!

LET HIM GO, YOU FOOL. IF YOU TRY TO STOP THEM, THEY'LL TAKE YOU TOO!

I'LL SEE YOU, ODIE, SOMETIME... SOMEWHERE

SO LONG
OLD FRIEND

NO!

COME ON. GET IN LINE!
WHAT FOR?

THERE'S A FAMILY COMING IN TO ADOPT A CAT OR A DOG. THIS COULD BE OUR WAY OUT

OUR WAY OUT...

ANTLER POLISH

LET'S SEE...

COME ON WILL YOU, HURRY UP

I'LL TAKE THAT ONE

ME?

SHE HAS GOOD TASTE

STOP
92

WELL, I SUPPOSE YOU BOYS HAD A BIG NIGHT, SINGING ON THE FENCE AND CHASING CARS

WHILE I SAT HOME AND WORRIED MYSELF SICK OVER YOU

I THOUGHT SO

HOME IS WHERE THEY UNDERSTAND YOU

-NEWS-

IT'S PATHETIC THE WAY SOME ANIMALS BEG AT THE TABLE

WHERE IS YOUR PRIDE ODIE?

OKAY, OKAY, HERE YOU GO BOY
NEW

NEWS

OH, VERY WELL, GARFIELD

NEWS

SPLAT!
NEWS

NEWS

I'M ONLY HUMAN!

An Interview with Garfield

Q: Garfield, congratulations on the success of your first television special! How do you feel?
A: Hungry!

Q: Do you think success has gone to your head?
A: It's hard to be humble when you're as great as I am.

Q: Why wasn't there any sex and violence in your special?
A: Nobody's perfect.

Q: How do you feel about commercials?
A: Too long to sit through; too short for a trip to the sandbox.

Q: Do you have any further comments?
A: Where's my Emmy?

GARFIELD
ON THE TOWN

BY: JIM DAVIS
and Lorenzo Music

GARFIELD
ON THE TOWN

GOOD MORNING, MORNING

WELL, I GUESS I'LL GET UP, WAKE JON AND EXERCISE

UNLESS, OF COURSE, THAT FLOOR IS COLD

I HATE COLD FLOORS

I'M NOT GETTING OUT OF BED IF THAT FLOOR IS THE SLIGHTEST BIT CHILLY

YIIII!
IT'S FREEZING!

TOO BAD

Z

I'M HUNGRY

CLOMP
CLOMP
CLOMP

HUNGRY, GARFIELD?

YOU GUESSED IT BUSTER!

OKEY DOKEY

FOOD

HERE YOU GO
BURP! NO THANKS. I COULDN'T POSSIBLY EAT ANOTHER BITE

BARK!

AND THEY SAY PETS
ARE THERAPEUTIC

SPROING!

SO THERE YOU ARE. WHERE'S ODIE?

POP!

BOYS, BOYS, BOYS. JUST LOOK AT THIS ROOM

WHAT AM I GOING TO DO WITH YOU TWO? CRUELTY TO ANIMALS COMES TO MIND...

A ONE WAY TICKET TO THE CITY POUND SEEMS LIKE A GOOD IDEA

RIGHT NOW EVEN TAXIDERMY SOUNDS TERRIFIC

I WORK AND SLAVE FOR YOU AND DO I GET ANY THANKS FOR IT? NOOO I DON'T. WHAT DO I GET?

A DEMOLITION DERBY IN MY LIVING ROOM!

YOU'RE HYPERACTIVE, GARFIELD, AND THAT'S NOT NORMAL FOR YOU. IT'S TIME FOR A TRIP TO THE VET

THE VET!

GARFIELD

GARFIELD!

QUIT PLAYING WITH THE POWER SEAT

NOW SIT STILL, GARFIELD

THAT'S A GOOD BOY

JON? WHAT HAPPENED?

HEY, WATCH IT!

CAT IN THE ROAD! CAREFUL! WOOPS! HEY!

WHEW!

WHEW!

I'M FREE. THIS IS GREAT... TOTALLY FREE

YOU KNOW, SOMEHOW I GET THE FEELING THIS IS NOT WHERE THE ACTION IS

LOST ST.
FOUND AVE.

BL + DS
CLAWS

BL + DS
CLAWS

ACTION! THIS COULD BE MY TIME TO HOWL!
CLAWS

AROOO!
CLAWS

WHAT'S HAPPENIN' BABY?
TAKE A HIKE JACK

AROOO!
CLAWS

HOW'S ABOUT YOU AND ME DOIN' SOMETHING BEAUTIFUL, DARLIN?
CAN IT, CREEP

AROOO!
CLAWS

HEY, HONEY, WHAT'S YOUR SIGN?
SUCK AIR, BOZO

AROOO!
BL + DS
CLAW

I MISS MY HOUSE
BL + DS
CLAWS

MAY I SPEAK WITH DR. WILSON, PLEASE?... YES, I'LL HOLD

WILSON

YIP!
WILSON

DR. WILSON
WILSON

HI, DOC, THIS IS JON ARBUCKLE, YOU KNOW, GARFIELD'S OWNER
GARFIELD, WHAT NOW?

WELL, HE'S BEEN GONE FOR A WHILE, AND I WAS AFRAID HE MIGHT HAVE BEEN HIT BY A CAR
IN THAT CASE, YOU WANT A TOW TRUCK

WELL, THANKS FOR YOUR CONCERN

BOY, IT'S STARTING TO GET DARK. NO SWEAT, I CAN TAKE CARE OF MYSELF. IN FACT IT MIGHT BE KIND OF FUN TO GET INTO A LITTLE RUMBLE JUST TO LOOSEN UP

JUST LET SOMEONE TRY SOMETHING. I'LL GIVE 'EM THE OL'... **HI-YA!**

YA-HA!

AHH... I KNEW IT WAS YOU ALL THE TIME. DON'T EVER DO THAT AGAIN, OKAY?... OKAY

YOU HUNGRY?

ME TOO. LET'S FIND A PLACE TO EAT

THIS LOOKS GOOD. GALVANIZED! NOT ONE OF THOSE CHEAP PLASTIC PLACES

BON APPÉTIT

PEEYEW!

AFTER YOU... OH NO, I INSIST, AFTER YOU

YOU'RE OUT OF YOUR TERRITORY, AIN'T YA FELLA?

HI!

THIS IS MY GARBAGE CAN
YOU MEAN YOU EAT HERE?

MY CONDOLENCES.
WELL, I'LL BE GOING NOW...

IT'S NOT THAT EASY...
PUFFBALL

DID YOU JUST CALL ME...
PUFFBALL?

OH, THAT OFFENDS YOU? I'M SORRY... LARDBALL
THAT DOES IT. I WAS THINKING ABOUT GETTING SOME EXERCISE

PIECE OF CAKE

THIS IS NOT GOOD

COME ON WILL YA?

WELL, SHADOW, I GUESS IT'S JUST YOU AND ME, LET'S TAKE 'EM

GOOD IDEA... WAIT FOR ME!

DO I KNOW YOU?

THINK BACK, GARFIELD

MOM?

MY LITTLE BOY

MY YOU'VE GOTTEN FAT
HEY

HELLO, WANT ADS? LOST AND FOUND PLEASE. HI, I WANT TO RUN AN AD. ...MISSING, A BEAUTIFUL ORANGE-STRIPED TABBY CAT OF THE LARGE BONED PERSUASION, ANSWERING TO THE NAME OF GARFIELD

WHEN FOUND HE'LL PROBABLY BE HUNGRY. HIS FAVORITE FOOD IS LASAGNA, BUT HE'LL TAKE ANY OTHER KIND OF PASTA DISH, SAY, DEEP-DISH CAVATINI...

UPON FINDING GARFIELD, PLEASE CONTACT JON ARBUCKLE AT 555-7722. A REWARD IS OFFERED... BY THE WAY, HOW MUCH WILL IT COST?

HOW MUCH?

WELL IN THAT CASE, HAVE IT READ, "LOST, FAT ORANGE-STRIPED CAT, REWARD." THANK YOU

GOOD MORNING, GARFIELD

OH, GOOD MORNING, MOM. FOR A MINUTE THERE I THOUGHT I WAS DREAMING

THIS IS REAL... BELIEVE ME

OO-EEE-AH-YAH!

MOM, IT'S BEEN JUST DRIVING ME CRAZY. WHERE ARE WE?

YOU'RE HOME, GARFIELD
HOME?

YES. THIS USED TO BE THE KITCHEN OF AN ITALIAN RESTAURANT

OH! OH! OH! I'M STARTING TO REMEMBER. THERE WAS A TABLE OVER THERE...

AND WAS THERE A STOVE OVER THERE? AND A BIG, FAT GUY WITH A MUSTACHE?
YOU DO REMEMBER

AND OVER THERE IS WHERE YOU WERE BORN

NOW I REMEMBER EVERYTHING

FOLLOW ME, GARFIELD
I WONDER WHERE WE'RE GOING

I THINK WE FOUND HIM!
OH BOY, OH BOY!

MUCH SMALLER THAN I REMEMBERED IT

THIS IS YOUR FAMILY, GARFIELD. COUSINS, MOSTLY
FAMILY?

GEE, THEY'RE SO SKINNY

DEAR, TIMES ARE TOUGH. EVEN FOR MOUSERS

MOUSERS?

YEECH!

GARFIELD, THIS IS YOUR COUSIN, SLY

HI, SLY, WHAT'S HAPPENING? HOW'S IT GOIN'? HOW YOU DOIN'?

DOESN'T SEEM TOO FRIENDLY
HE'S ON DUTY, DEAR. SLY IS OUR WATCH CAT

WATCH CAT, HUH? HEY, SLY, WATCH THIS!

FUN FAMILY, I CAN'T WAIT TO...

HACK
COUGH
HACK

THAT'S RAOUL... YOUR BROTHER

OH WOW, MAN. THAT'S THE FIRST TIME I EVER SEEN ONE OF THOSE. PART CAT, PART HOUSE, YOU MUST BE ONE OF THEM HOUSE-CATS

HEY, THAT WAS PRETTY GOOD,... HOUSE-CAT

HYSTERICAL, SO LISTEN, EVERYTHING COOL? MAYBE WE COULD HANG OUT SOMETIME

PARDON ME, BRO. I GOTTA CATCH A FEW MORE Z'S

RAOUL ISN'T WELL
I'M NOT DOING THAT GOOD MYSELF

GARFIELD, THIS IS YOUR GRANDFATHER. FATHER, I'D LIKE YOU TO MEET GARFIELD

HI, PLEASED TO...

YOU'RE SOFT BOY, TOO PROUD TO WORK FOR A LIVING ?

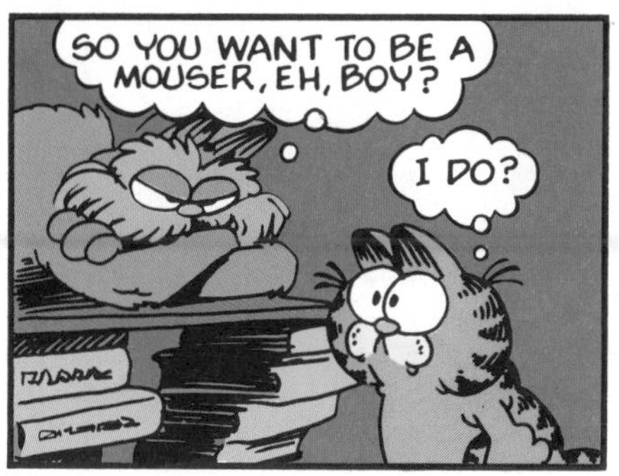
SO YOU WANT TO BE A MOUSER, EH, BOY ?
I DO?

WE HAVE A TRADITION TO UPHOLD, MY BOY, YOUR FATHER, YOUR GREAT-GRANDFATHER, YOUR GREAT-GREAT-GRANDFATHER... WE'VE ALWAYS BEEN MOUSERS

ARE THEY HERE?

THEY DROP IN FROM TIME TO TIME... GARFIELD, YOU COME FROM A LONG LINE OF BACHELORS

OH

PREPARE FOR THE GAMES!

LET THE GAME BEGIN!

WHAT'S HAPPENING?
THIS IS YOUR INITIATION, MAN. THE ULTIMATE TEST OF YOUR CATHOOD

WHAT AM I SUPPOSED TO DO?
WELL, OFFHAND, I'D SAY THAT YOU'RE SUPPOSED TO CATCH THAT MOUSE

YOU KNOW, I'M NOT REALLY UP FOR THIS, WOULD ANYONE MIND IF WE PUT THIS OFF UNTIL AFTER LUNCH?

THAT IS LUNCH

OH

YOU KNOW...THIS IS REALLY UNFAIR. BACK HOME I'M FAMOUS FOR THIS KIND OF STUFF. UH... DON'T YOU HAVE ANYTHING BIGGER?

BIGGER?

YEAH... MORE OF A CHALLENGE

WELL... NOW THAT YOU MENTION IT... BRING ON THE TRAINING MOUSE

THIS END UP

MINNIE
NOW THAT'S WHAT I CALL A MOUSE!

COME ON, BOY

YUM-YUM, EAT 'UM UP

EAT 'UM UP, SURE. DOES ANYBODY HAVE ANY SALT? JUST KIDDING. SERIOUSLY, THIS IS GOING TO BE FUN. LOOKS LIKE A GOOD YEAR FOR MOUSE. OKAY, OKAY, I'LL EAT IT, BIG DEAL

INCOMING!

TOPSIDE! TOPSIDE! CAT YOUR BATTLE STATIONS!

GET READY TO FIGHT, DEAR

FIGHT? FIGHT WHAT? I HATE FIGHTING. THERE'S ALREADY TOO MUCH FIGHTING IN THE WORLD

CUT THE PHILOSOPHY, CHUBBY, MOVE!

I'M GONNA LET YOU GO THIS TIME
MINNIE

WHATEVER
MICKEY

THANKS
ANY TIME

WHAT'S HAPPENING?
IT'S THE CLAWS

THE CLAWS?

WE HAVEN'T HAD TROUBLE WITH THEM FOR A LONG TIME. I WONDER WHAT THEY WANT?

I THINK I CAN GUESS

WHAT DO YOU WANT?

LARDBALL!

THEY WANT SOMEONE CALLED, "LARDBALL"

LARDBALL?

WHO'S LARDBALL?

YEAH. THAT FAT ORANGE-STRIPED WIMP. WE KNOW HE'S IN THERE, SO WE'LL MAKE IT REAL SIMPLE. YOU THROW OUT LARDBALL, WE LEAVE, YOU DON'T, WE LEVEL THE PLACE

WE FIGHT!

WE FIGHT. HEY, GREAT!

RUM-BLE!

AAAARRRGHH!

HEY GARFIELD, WATCH THIS

LOOK ISN'T THAT HALLEY'S COMET?

NOT BAD

I GUESS WE SHOWED THEM, HUH? THEY WON'T TRY THAT AGAIN. NOT WITH THIS FAMILY

LARDBALL, GO HOME

WHAT CAN I DO?

NO, PLEASE, DON'T ASK ME TO STAY. I REALLY, HAVE TO GO

I'M SORRY I LET YOU DOWN, MOM

THERE'S NOTHING TO BE SORRY ABOUT, GARFIELD. NOT ALL OF US ARE CUT OUT TO BE MOUSERS
I'LL SAY

GARFIELD, THIS IS REALLY FOR THE BEST. YOU WOULDN'T SURVIVE HERE. YOU HAVE A GOOD LIFE, AN EASY LIFE. WE ALL ENVY YOU

I'LL MISS YOU

I'LL BE WITH YOU, GARFIELD. IF YOU EVER NEED ME, I'LL BE THERE, GO DEAR... IT'S STARTING TO GET DARK

I LOVE YOU

I LOVE YOU TOO, MOM

SUE
CLAWS

I'M HUNGRY. I COULD WASTE AWAY TO NORMAL. NAH, I'M TOO TIRED TO BE HUNGRY. NAH, I'M TOO SCARED TO BE TIRED

MAYBE IF I WHISTLE I WON'T BE SCARED
FFFF

WHAT AM I DOING... CATS CAN'T WHISTLE. I GUESS I'LL JUST LIE DOWN HERE... AND HOPE FOR SOMETHING BIG TO FALL ON ME

I CAN SEE THE HEADLINE NOW. "EXTREMELY GOOD LOOKING CAT TOTALED IN PIANO CRASH." I'M GONNA MISS ME. NOW I'M LONELY

WHAT MORE COULD POSSIBLY GO WRONG?

NICE TOUCH

HEY!

HEY!!!

JON!

LAUNDRY

BOB'S
BAR & GRILL

BARK
BARK

GARFIELD, IS THAT YOU?

THANK YOU... THAT WAS ENOUGH FUN FOR ONE DAY

LASAGNA!

HOME, JON

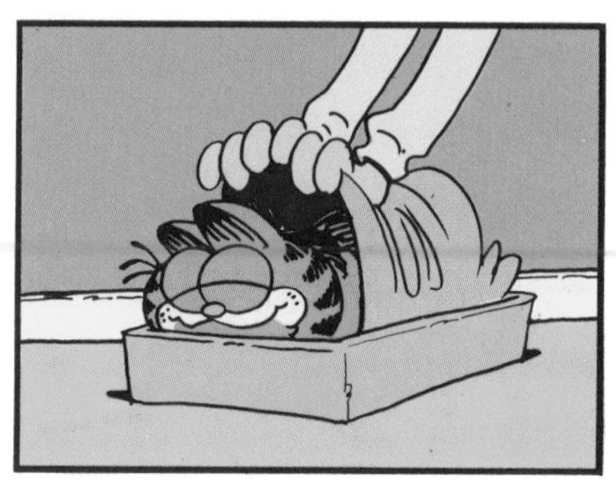

URF!

YES ODIE, YOU FOUND ME

YOU LOOK BAD, GARFIELD. WHAT A NIGHT. DID THAT REALLY HAPPEN? DID I REALLY MEET MY...? DID SHE REALLY...?

NAAA...

THANKS, MOM... FOR EVERYTHING

Garfield Animated
Z

Garfield

GETS A LIFE

BY: JIM DAVIS

SIGH

SIGH

THONK

SIGH

FAP

SIGH

TOING
TOING

SIGH
SIGH

MORNING, ODIE
MORNING, ODIE

BARK

THERE YOU GO, BOY

SIGH
SIGH

WELL, I GUESS I'LL GO SHOWER AND SHAVE

THANKS FOR SHARING THAT WITH ME, JON
YES, FOLKS, THIS IS MY LIFE. WHILE IT MAY LOOK VITAL AND STIMULATING, IT REALLY ISN'T. THAT'S BECAUSE JON'S A BORE
HE REALLY NEEDS TO GET A LIFE AND I INTEND TO HELP HIM FIND ONE
UNLESS, OF COURSE, THERE IS SOMETHING GOOD ON T.V.

AH, TIME FOR MY FAVORITE SHOW..."YUKON STINKY"

"THIS WEEK, YUKON STINKY INSULTS A POLAR BEAR"

I CAN'T MISS THAT

JON'S LIFE CAN WAIT

LATER...
THAT SHOULD BE ENOUGH STIMULATION FOR ONE MORNING
CLICK

ONE, TWO, THREE, FOUR...

FIVE, SIX, SEVEN, EIGHT...

NINE, TEN, ELEVEN, TWELVE...

THIRTEEN, FOURTEEN, FIFTEEN

141, 142, 143, 144, .. GARFIELD, DID YOU KNOW THE BEDROOM CEILING HAS 144 TILES
THE LIVING ROOM HAS 214

I'M BORED

WHY DON'T YOU ORGANIZE YOUR SOCK DRAWER?

I'D ORGANIZE MY SOCK DRAWER, BUT I JUST ORGANIZED IT LAST NIGHT
I'LL BE THE JUDGE OF THAT

WHOA. I'M IMPRESSED. ALL NICELY TUCKED AND SORTED BY COLOR AND SIZE

THESE ARE THE WINTER SOCKS. THE SUMMER ONES ARE IN THE OTHER DRAWER

HERE WE HAVE YOUR NATURAL FIBER SOCKS, HERE'S YOUR MAN-MADE FIBER SOCKS, AND OF COURSE, HERE YOU'VE GOT YOUR BLENDS

YOU KNOW WHAT, GARFIELD?

YOU NEED A LIFE
I NEED A LIFE

THERE'S MORE TO LIFE THAN SOCKS

THERE'S UNDERWEAR

THERE'S A BIGGER WORLD OUT THERE BEYOND THIS SOCK DRAWER

AND I'M GONNA LIVE IT
SLAM!

HAVEN'T YOU GOT A LIFE, YET??

WHAT ARE YOU WAITING FOR? DO I HAVE TO DO EVERYTHING AROUND HERE?

"HOW TO MAKE FRIENDS AND FOOL THE REST"
HOW TO MAKE FRIENDS AND FOOL THE REST

A BOOK ON SINCERITY

I FORGOT I HAD THIS BOOK. HEY, THIS CHAPTER ON GETTING DATES IS JUST THE TICKET

GREAT. READ IT AND GIVE ME A FULL REPORT. THE SOONER YOU GET HAPPY WITH YOUR LIFE, THE SOONER I CAN GET BACK TO MINE

HUMANS...NEVER SATISFIED... IF ONLY THEY'D LEARN TO BE CONTENT WITH THE SIMPLE THINGS IN LIFE... LIKE LASAGNA...

A GOOD NAP...

FAMILY...

DOG BREATH PEE-YEW!
HUH?

Club
Club
Club

IT SAYS HERE, A SINGLES CLUB IS JUST THE TICKET

...FOR A HAPPENIN' GUY LIKE ME

"HEY-THERE-WOULD-YOU-LIKE-TO-DANCE-WITH-ME?"

SURE, WHY NOT?

YES!
YES!

DID YOU HEAR THAT, GARFIELD? SHE WANTS TO DANCE WITH ME

IT'S A MIRACLE

COME, MY DEAR, LET'S CUT A RUG

HEY, BUDDY...
DISCO IS
DEAD
WHAT?

WHEN?

SIGH

BOY, YOU LEARN A DANCE THEN ZANGO! FOURTEEN YEARS LATER THEY CHANGE IT

GO FIGURE

ONLY LOW HEAT
OUT OF ORDER
REPORT ANY PROBLEMS TO MANAGER- (GOOD LUCK FINDING HIM
OVERLOAD
-KEEP- CHILDREN OUT OF MACHINES
CHANGE
IT SAYS HERE A LAUNDROMAT IS A GREAT PLACE TO MEET CHICKS

LOOKS LIKE A GOOD PLACE TO TAKE A NAP

CLEAN CHICKS!

PARDON ME, I COULDN'T HELP BUT NOTICE YOUR FRILLY LITTLE, UH

...TUTU THING THERE. ARE YOU A BALLERINA?

WHY, YES I AM

AND I COULDN'T HELP BUT NOTICE YOUR TEDDY BEAR BOXER SHORTS

ARE YOU A DWEEB?

WHY, YES HE IS

PARDON ME, LADIES. I SEEM TO HAVE LOST MY OLYMPIC SWIMMING MEDALS AROUND HERE SOMEWHERE

I MIGHT HAVE LOST THEM OVER THERE...

OR OVER THERE

I CAN'T REMEMBER

OH WELL
I THINK I'LL DO SOME PUSH-UPS

OUT OF MY WAY, WIMP

OOPS!

CRASH!
POW!

THIS MAY COME AS A SURPRISE TO YOU, GARFIELD, BUT I'M JUST NOT VERY GOOD AT GETTING A DATE

NAAAWWWW...!! GWAAAANNNN... YOU'RE PUTTING ME ON

HELLO THERE!
WHAP!

DON'T FLATTER YOURSELF
STRIKE ONE

MAYBE I OUGHTA JUST FORGET ABOUT MEETING ANYONE...EVER. MAYBE I'LL BECOME A NUN
AS LONG AS IT GETS YOU OUT OF THE HOUSE

HI THERE

TAKE A HIKE
NO THANKS, I JUST TOOK ONE

STRIKE TWO

WHAT IS IT, GARFIELD? IS IT MY BREATH? MY LOOKS? MY PERSONALITY?

WHY CAN'T I...

YO THERE!

BUZZ OFF
BUZZ

OOH, STRIKE THREE. YOU'RE OUTTA HERE, BIG GUY

AND NOW, THIS WORD FROM OUR SPONSOR

FRIENDS...
ARE YOU LONELY?

BORED? A LOSER? IS YOUR IDEA OF A FUN SATURDAY NIGHT SITTING AT HOME WATCHING TV
...WITH YOUR CAT?

PPPTTT!

ARE YOU SO BORING THAT YOU COULD MAKE CHEESE YAWN?

ARE YOU SO OUT OF TOUCH THAT YOU THINK DISCO IS STILL "IN"?

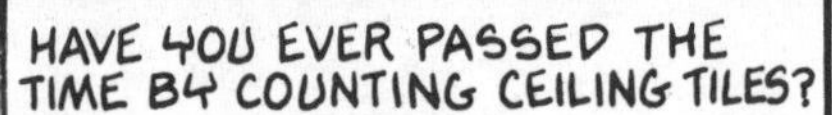
HAVE YOU EVER PASSED THE TIME BY COUNTING CEILING TILES?

COMPARED TO YOU DOES A SLUG SEEM HYPERACTIVE?

WELL FRIEND, IF THIS IS YOU, CHEER UP! THERE IS HELP FOR YOU AT THE...

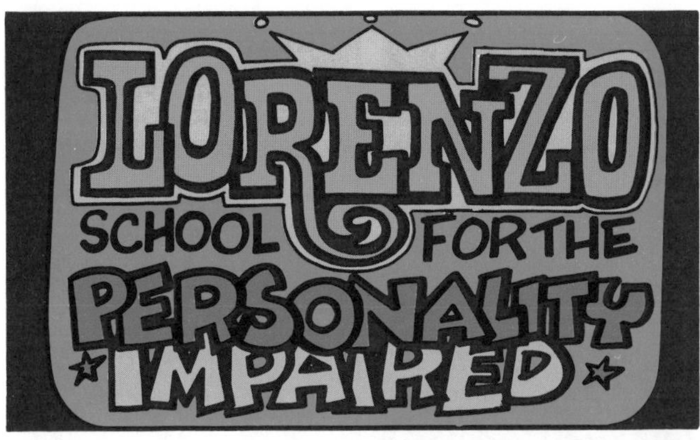
LORENZO
SCHOOL FOR THE
PERSONALITY
IMPAIRED

THAT'S RIGHT. AT "LORENZO'S SCHOOL FOR THE PERSONALITY IMPAIRED" WE CAN SHOW YOU HOW TO GET A LIFE
L

WE CAN TAKE EVEN THE MOST HUMDRUM, UNINTERESTING, AND TIRESOME BORE
BEFORE

... AND TURN HIM INTO SOMEONE VITAL, ENERGETIC, AND SELF-ASSURED
AFTER

WE'LL SHOW YOU HOW TO MAKE FRIENDS,

HOW TO DO IMPRESSIONS,

HOW TO HAVE FUN

AT "LORENZO'S SCHOOL FOR THE PERSONALITY IMPAIRED" WE'VE GOT A PROVEN TRACK RECORD

I WONDER IF THEY COULD HELP ME?
REMEMBER FRIENDS, OUR MOTTO IS...

"IF YOU CAN GET A PULSE,
...YOU CAN GET A LIFE."

MAYBE THEY'LL TAKE YOU ANYWAY

LORENZO'S
SCHOOL FOR THE
PERSONALITY IMPAIRED

HELLO, HELLO. WELCOME TO "LORENZO'S SCHOOL FOR THE PERSONALITY IMPAIRED." MAY I HELP YOU?

UH, YES, I'M HERE TO GET A LIFE

UH, I MEAN I HAVE A LIFE, BUT IT'S BORING

WELL, IT'S NOT THAT IT'S BORING SO MUCH

YES, I SEE. WE'LL WANT TO START YOU RIGHT OUT IN ROOM 1A
RECPT'Y

THAT'S "HOW TO MAKE A GOOD FIRST IMPRESSION." DOWN THE HALL, FIRST DOOR ON THE RIGHT

HAVE A NICE LIFE
I'D SETTLE FOR A NICE LUNCH
RECPTY

I WONDER IF THIS IS THE PLACE

12...13...14
5...6...7
98...99... 100
43...44... 45
78...79...80
22...23...24
31...32...33
122...123...124

YEAH, THIS IS THE PLACE

HOW DO YOU DO? MY NAME IS LORENZO

WHAT IS YOUR NAME?

JON, JON ARBUCKLE

AND THIS IS MY...ER...ARE YOU THE LORENZO IN THE COMMERCIAL?

IN PERSON

GEE, ON T.V. YOU SOUNDED SO... SO...

SO WHAT?

SO ALIVE

OH, THAT WAS A LIP SYNC. YOU KNOW, MY BODY, CHARLTON HESTON'S VOICE

I SEE

ONWARD AND UPWARD, SHALL WE? HAVE A SEAT, MR. ARBUCKLE

GOOD MORNING, CLASS

THE FIRST STEP TO BECOMING A VITAL PERSON...

IS TO MAKE A GOOD FIRST IMPRESSION

NOW, "HOW MIGHT I DO THAT?" YOU MIGHT ASK

YOU DO THAT BY WALKING RIGHT UP TO THEM...

LOOK THEM RIGHT IN THE...

EYE...

GIVING THEM A FIRM HANDSHAKE...

...AND SAYING, "HELLO, MY NAME IS SO AND SO." EVERYONE TURN TO THE PERSON NEXT TO YOU AND GIVE IT A TRY

HELLO, MY NAME IS...

HELLO, MY NAME IS...

HELLO, MY NAME IS...
HELLO, MY NAME IS...

HELLO, MY NAME IS...
HELLO, MY NAME IS...

HELLO, MY NAME IS JON

HI, MY NAME IS MONA

HELLO, MY NAME IS GARFIELD. YOU'VE PROBABLY NOTICED...

WAS THAT OKAY?

WAS WHAT OKAY?

MY FIRST IMPRESSION

I REALLY HAVE NO IDEA WHAT I'M DOING

OH GOOD

HUH?
NEITHER DO I

HOW WAS MINE?

YOUR WHAT?
MY FIRST IMPRESSION

FINE... I GUESS

YOU GUESS?! I KNEW IT!

WHAT?
I HAVE SOMETHING BETWEEN MY TEETH, DON'T I?

NO, YOUR TEETH ARE FINE, SEE?!
SEE WHAT?

I'M BLOWING IT! I'M MAKING A LOUSY FIRST IMPRESSION
NO, YOU'RE NOT... I GUESS

YEAH, WHAT DO WE KNOW?

HEE HEE HEE
HEE HEE HEE

OKAY CLASS, ONWARD AND UPWARD! THE SECOND PART OF TODAY'S LESSON IS LEARNING TO DRESS FOR SUCCESS!

HEY, I'M NAKED!!!

IN ALL MODESTY, I MUST CONFESS, IN SOME CIRCLES...

I AM CONSIDERED A FASHION PLATE, IF YOU WILL

HEE-HEE
HEE
HEE
HEE
HEE
HEE

LET ME SHARE A FEW OF MY FASHION SECRETS WITH YOU

L

LOOK AND LEARN

RULE NUMBER ONE:
NOTICE HOW I HAVE COORDINATED MY JACKET LINING
...WITH MY SOCKS

ER...WELL, MY LEFT ONE AT ANY RATE
WHEN IT COMES TO COLOR, I SAY WHY WEAR ALL THE SAME COLOR
YOUR ENSEMBLE SHOULD BE A VIRTUAL SMORGASBORD FOR THE EYES

NOTICE HOW I'VE ACCENTED MY GREEN TWEED SLACKS
... WITH THIS PLAID JACKET
... AND THIS STRING TIE

I'M SO SHY
ME TOO

YOU'RE NOT SHY
YES, I AM

NO YOU'RE NOT. YOU'RE LIKE THAT GUY ON THE BEACH YESTERDAY
WHAT GUY?

OH, JUST SOME GUY. HE WAS WALKING AROUND FLEXING HIS MUSCLES

...AND LOOKING FOR HIS OLYMPIC SWIMMING MEDALS
HEE HEE

NOTHING IMPRESSES PEOPLE MORE THAN WHEN YOU SPEAK IN A FOREIGN LANGUAGE
L

BUT YOU DON'T REALLY HAVE TO LEARN A LANGUAGE...

IF YOU CAN SOUND LIKE YOU SPEAK IT

PEOPLE ARE REALLY IMPRESSED IF YOU CAN SPEAK FRENCH OR IF YOU CAN SOUND FRENCH

FOR EXAMPLE, "JE PARLE EN FRANCAIS"

OOOOHHHH!

LE IMPRESSIVE, NO?

YOU KNOW, I'VE HAD JUST ABOUT ENOUGH SOPHISTICATION FOR ONE DAY. HOW 'BOUT YOU?

OUI, MON AMI

HEY, YOU, MONSIEUR DUMB GUY, REMEMBER ME? WHAT AM I? CHOPPED LIVER? DUCK PATÉ? LIVERWURST? BOY, AM I HUNGRY

IT'S BEEN A WONDERFUL DAY, JON. CLASS WAS GREAT AND DINNER WAS FUN

BUT MOST OF ALL I'VE REALLY ENJOYED TALKING TO YOU

UNTIL I MET YOU, I THOUGHT I WAS THE ONLY PERSON IN THE WORLD TO GET MY TONGUE CAUGHT IN AN ELEVATOR DOOR

I'VE REALLY ENJOYED TALKING TO YOU TOO, MONA, AND WE DIDN'T HAVE TO SPEAK FRENCH

WHAT?
THINK ABOUT IT

WE HAD A WONDERFUL EVENING WITHOUT HAVING TO RELY ON ANYTHING WE LEARNED IN CLASS TODAY

DO YOU KNOW I'VE NEVER BEEN ABLE TO OPEN UP TO ANYONE LIKE THIS BEFORE

...OTHER THAN MY CAT, THAT IS

"OTHER THAN MY CAT, THAT IS"

"MY CAT"

YESTERDAY, I HAD A NAME. I WAS HIS BOSOM BUDDY, HIS CONFIDANT

TODAY, I'M HIS CAT

I CAN'T BELIEVE IT

JON'S ACTUALLY MET SOMEONE WHO LIKES HIM

AND IT'S NOT EVEN HIS MOTHER

Z

JUST
MARRIED
THUD!

PHEW!

OH NO! POOR JON! HE DOESN'T KNOW WHAT HE'S GETTING INTO. I MUST STOP HIM BEFORE HE MULTIPLIES!

THEN IN MY SENIOR YEAR... WHA?!!
GARFIELD?! WHAT ARE YOU DOING?

JON, YOU DON'T KNOW WHAT YOU'RE DOING

WHAT A SWEET CAT
DON'T LISTEN TO HER, JON! SHE'S TRYING TO GET TO YOU THROUGH ME!

WOULD YOU LIKE ME TO SCRATCH BEHIND YOUR EARS?
OH! THAT'S GOOD

SHE'S VERY GOOD, JON. ONCE SHE HAS ME IN HER CLUTCHES SHE'LL...

PERHAPS JUST A LITTLE BIT BEHIND THIS EAR

JON, LISTEN CAREFULLY. THIS IS ALL A...

JUST A LITTLE LOWER, PLEASE... THIS IS ALL A SINISTER PLOT TO GET YOU TO... OH YES! NOW...

ACHOOO!

OH...EXCUSE ME
ARE YOU OKAY?

I'M FINE, REALLY. IT'S JUST THAT I'M... THAT I'M...

ACHOO!

ALLERGIC TO CACHOO!

OH, FOR A MINUTE THERE I THOUGHT YOU SAID YOU WERE ALLERGIC TO CATS!

I... I AM...
ACHOO!
OH, NO!

AW, TOO BAD. WHAT A SHAME. SHE WAS SO CUTE. AND SUCH A GOOD EAR SCRATCHER, TOO

COME ALONG, JON

SAY GOODBYE TO YOUR LITTLE FRIEND. IT'S TIME TO FIX DINNER, ANYWAY

WELL, WHAT ARE YOU WAITING ON?

THIS IS TERRIBLE

I'M SORRY, JON, SNIFF
CAN'T YOU TAKE SHOTS FOR YOUR ALLERGY?

THEY DON'T DO ME ANY GOOD
WHAT CAN I DO?

YOU CAN CHUCK HER ON THE CHIN, SAY, "IT'S BEEN NICE KNOWIN' YOU KID"...

AND SEND HER ON HER WAY

WHAT IF I SHAVED MY CAT?

HEY, WHOA... TIME-OUT!

OH, MONA, YOU'RE SO SWEET
JON! WHAT'S THE MATTER WITH YOU?

THERE'S SOMETHING TO BE SAID FOR SENIORITY

CAN WE STILL SEE EACH OTHER SOMETIME, JON?

I'D LIKE THAT

NOT WITHOUT A CHAPERON. JON'S MORE THAN A FRIEND TO ME... HE'S MY MEAL TICKET

COME ON. I'LL TAKE YOU HOME

HANG ON! WAIT FOR ME!

VROOOM!
-INDIANA-
PAWS·KH36

YOU'RE NOT LEAVING ME BEHIND
SCHTUNK
SCHTUNK
-INDIANA-
PAWS·KH36

I SAW THIS ON A FREEWAY ONCE